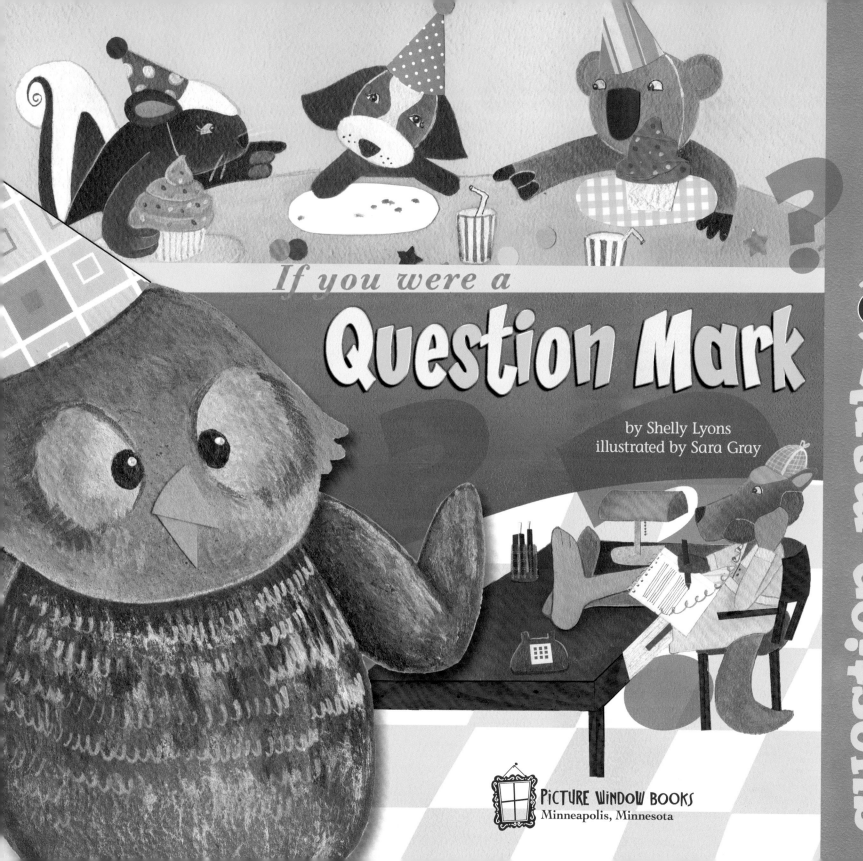

If you were a

Question Mark

by Shelly Lyons
illustrated by Sara Gray

PICTURE WINDOW BOOKS
Minneapolis, Minnesota

question mark (?.) a punctuation
mark used at the end of a question

Editors: Christianne Jones and Jill Kalz
Designer: Tracy Davies
Page Production: Melissa Kes
Art Director: Nathan Gassman
Editorial Director: Nick Healy
The illustrations in this book were created with acrylics.

Picture Window Books
151 Good Counsel Drive
P.O. Box 669
Mankato, MN 56002-0669
877-845-8392
www.picturewindowbooks.com

Printed in the United States of America.

 All books published by Picture Window Books
are manufactured with paper containing at least
10 percent post-consumer waste.

Library of Congress Cataloging-in-Publication Data
Lyons, Shelly.
If you were a question mark / by Shelly Lyons ;
illustrated by Sara Gray.
p. cm. — (Word Fun)
Includes index.
ISBN 978-1-4048-5323-2 (library binding)
ISBN 978-1-4048-5324-9 (paperback)
1. English language—Punctuation—Juvenile literature.
2. English language—Interrogative—Juvenile literature.
3. Birthday parties—Juvenile literature. 4. Mystery—
Juvenile literature. 5. Language arts (Primary)
I. Gray, Sara, ill. II. Title.
PE1450.L96 2009
428.2—dc22   2008039316

Looking for question marks? Watch for the **BIG** marks throughout the book.

Special thanks to our advisers for their expertise:

Rosemary G. Palmer, Ph.D., Department of Literacy
College of Education, Boise State University

Terry Flaherty, Ph.D., Professor of English
Minnesota State University, Mankato

If you were a
question mark ...

3

"Who can help us solve this mystery?"

If you were a question mark, you would replace the period at the end of a sentence that asks a question.

If you were a question mark, you could ask for directions.

"How do I get to Sophie's house?"

8

"Can you please show me to the kitchen?"

9

If you were a question mark, you could ask for the facts.

"When did Sophie's strawberry cupcake disappear?"

If you were a question mark, you could ask how someone feels.

"Is Sophie upset?"

If you were a question mark, you could ask for help.

"Can you please hold this magnifying glass?"

"Will you please shine this flashlight on Sophie's plate?"

"Sophie, can you help me look for paw prints?"

If you were a question mark, you could follow a number or a date that is not certain.

How many cupcakes did we start with? Six?

How many are left? Two? Three?

17

If you were a question mark, you would make it clear that a statement is actually a question.

Ella is the thief? No, not her.

Dalton doesn't like strawberry? True. He loves chocolate.

Sam wasn't hungry? That's right. He said he was full.

19

If you were a question mark, you could ask the really important questions.

Do you see frosting paw prints?

Why is that box shaking?

Is that strawberry frosting on Jasper's nose?

Quick Review

A question mark replaces a period at the end of a sentence that asks a question.
   Do you like solving mysteries?

Question marks can help you learn which way to go.
   Where is Sophie's house? Should I turn left or right?

Question marks can help you figure out the facts.
   Who? What? When? Where? How? Why?

A question mark can help you find out more about other people.
   Are you sad because the cupcake is gone?
   Jasper is the thief?

Question marks follow dates or numbers that are not certain.
   1992? 28?

Fun with Question Marks

Gather a group of friends. Choose one person to be "It," and have that person leave the room. While he is gone, choose an object in the room. For example, you might pick a clock, a pencil, or a light bulb.

When "It" comes back, have him guess what the object is by asking up to 20 questions. Only questions with yes or no answers are allowed. If he guesses correctly, someone else becomes "It." If not, he stays "It" for the next game.

Glossary

period—a punctuation mark used at the end of most sentences and abbreviations

punctuation—marks used to make written language clear

question mark—a punctuation mark used at the end of a question

replace—to take the place of

statement—something stated, or said

Index

To Learn More

More Books to Read

Cooper, Barbara. *Quincy Question Mark*. Milwaukee: Gareth Stevens Pub., 2005.

Donohue, Moira Rose. *Penny and the Punctuation Bee*. Morton Grove, Ill.: Albert Whitman & Co., 2008.

Pulver, Robin. *Punctuation Takes a Vacation*. New York: Holiday House, 2003.

Salzmann, Mary Elizabeth. *Question Mark*. Edina, Minn.: ABDO Pub., 2001.

On the Web

FactHound offers a safe, fun way to find educator-approved Internet sites.

Here's what you do:
1. Visit *www.facthound.com*
2. Choose your grade level.
3. Begin your search.

This book's ID number is 9781404853232

Look for all of the books in the Word Fun: Punctuation series:

If You Were a Comma
If You Were a Period
If You Were a Question Mark
If You Were an Apostrophe
If You Were an Exclamation Point
If You Were Quotation Marks